## Serene Scenes

## Outside the Lines

## Direct to Paper

## Direct to Stamp

## Magic With Markers

## Easy Elements

# Letter to Readers

As an illustrator of rubber stamps, I find it easy to come up with ideas for how to use my images with inky techniques that will best showcase them. However, continually coming up with new and fresh layouts for cards doesn't always happen so easily. Layering shapes, textures and colored mats—and knowing how to balance them in an arrangement that is pleasing to the eye—is an extremely important part of designing cards and something that most beginners struggle with. Not finding that balance often leads to frustration, a less than successful end product or not finishing the project at all. While there are no hard "rules" in creating art, it is important for a card maker to like his or her work and to have, if one wishes, the confidence to move beyond creating single-layer cards in clean and simple designs.

With ten years of stamping and card-making experience, I've developed or adopted many go-to layouts that I love and fall back on for inspiration when I am stumped for a design idea. In wanting to make this creative process easier for new card makers, as well as provide inspiration and faster mass production for experts, I began developing stamp sets with large frame images for Gina K. Designs. These sets, designed specifically with A2-size (4¼ x 5½ inch) cards in mind, can be stamped in one step to fill an entire card front—layout complete. What makes these frames even more versatile is the option of rotating them in a portrait or landscape orientation, creating two to four different looks. Each image also contains open space intended for greetings, stamped focal points or even precious photos, taking the guesswork out of where these elements should go. While the frames provide great consistency, there are still many ways to make these cards as unique as the individual receiving your card.

Over the last four years, I've released frame sets in styles for every stamper: whimsical shapes, clean graphic lines and ever-popular florals, many of which you'll recognize from my first book, *A Year of Flowers*, and its companion stamp set of the same name. Additionally, whether you love stamping with bold stamps, line art images or a combination of both, the sets used for this book cover the entire range of stamp techniques with no limit to what can be achieved. Because of their ease of use and gorgeous results, these frame sets continue to be some of our customers' favorites, mine included. They are by far the inkiest and most beloved stamps in my vast collection—the ones for which I never seem to run out of ideas. With a framework for my card base out of the way, I am free to let my imagination run wild with the rest. As a busy mom of two very busy children, anything that makes work and crafting faster for me is a true blessing!

I'm so excited to share the ideas and samples on the following pages with you and pray that you'll love these images and this approach to creating stamped cards as much as I do. What's not to love about fun, fast and fabulous?

I'd like to extend a heartfelt thanks to all our Gina K. Designs and *StampTV* fans and customers who have fallen in love with these frame sets—this book is for you. Thanks also to friends, family, mentors and praying saints who have supported, advised, encouraged and lifted up prayers for me all along the way.

God bless!
Melanie

# Fabulous
# STAMPED FRAMES™

## Creative Greeting Card Designs & Inspiration

## Splendid Spotlights

## Pretty Pencils

## Paper Piecing

## Faux Paper Piecing

## Cool Color Blocks

## Terrific Two Steps

# Author Bio

## Melanie Muenchinger

photo copyright © Marty Eisenberger

Melanie began stamping and card making in 2003, but has had a lifelong love affair with paper crafting. In 2008, she started working as a senior designer and illustrator for Gina K. Designs. To date, she has created over 60 stamp sets exclusively for Gina K. Designs, with sets ranging from clean graphic lines to realistic nature images, to whimsical animals and decorative elements. She was one of the original Dirty Dozen designers for Splitcoaststampers, and her published design work and tutorials can be found in the pages of *CardMaker*, *Crafts 'n' Things* and *Scrap & Stamp* magazines.

Melanie's first book, *A Year of Flowers*, which uses her stamp set of the same name, came out in January of 2012 and features tutorials for 36 all-occasion cards. The A Year of Flowers stamp set is one of Gina K.'s best-selling sets, and has been featured on PBS and in various crafting publications. The book has received rave reviews and has brought a new audience to Gina K. Designs stamps and store, for which their team is extremely grateful. The success of *A Year of Flowers* and the enthusiasm of its readers for tutorials and designs specific to Melanie's stamps made offering a follow-up book for her frame stamp sets an absolute must.

Melanie lives in Austin, Texas, with her husband Paul and two sons, Jonathan and William, and is grateful to be a stay-at-home mom, first, who also gets to draw and play with stamps and paper for a living. Melanie counts herself blessed by the opportunity to write this second book for Annie's. You can check out more of her past work and ongoing projects, tutorials and inspiration for all of her stamp sets, as well as those by other fabulous Gina K. Designs illustrators, on her blog "Hands, Head and Heart"—www.melaniemuenchinger.blogspot.com.

# Getting Started

Okay, you're here, so let's get stamping! If you are new to card making with stamps, there are a few basic supplies you'll need: stamps, ink, paper, adhesives and cutting tools. All of these general crafting materials can be found at any local craft store. To make it easy for you to find the supplies you'll need for these tutorials and projects, almost all products used are available online at Gina K. Designs. The materials lists for each project included in this book will help you decide what additional supplies you will need. If you don't already own the frame stamps, you will definitely want to add at least one or two of those to your stamp supply. A complete list of sources for products is included in the Buyer's Guide on page 64.

## The Stamps

Each stamp set featured in these projects is from Gina K. Designs and includes a beautiful frame, which will help you create a perfect greeting card layout every time. These sets include year-round greetings and additional images designed to complement the frame. These elements can also be used individually as focal points or to create patterns. Each chapter will showcase step-by-step tutorials with photos and instructions to demonstrate specific techniques, and variations of those techniques will be exhibited in the inspiration projects. Each of the seven frame sets featured in this book is described below, along with suggestions of the techniques they are best suited for.

If you love coloring or designs that require less stamping:

**Arranged with Love** includes an intricate floral frame with an open space for adding one of eight sentiments which cover year-round occasions. Using this set is like sending a gorgeous bouquet with a personal message. The flowers and leaves are the same size and shape as images featured in A Year of Flowers stamp set, making it easy to stamp single blooms to pop up over the frame for added color and dimension.

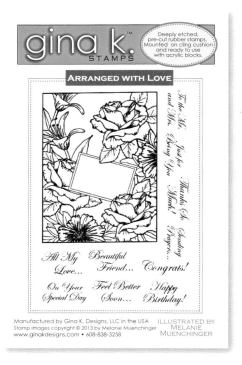

If you love inky techniques, more involved stamping or creating your own backgrounds:

**Inspiration Mosaic**, designed with a grid frame, works as a four-way sketch and includes geometric elements that can be used individually or to modify the frame. A variety of sentiments in a clean, modern font fit into the open boxes in any orientation. The clean lines in this frame complement any design or images of any style. Stamp the frame over a picture or other images, and it becomes an interesting collection of canvases.

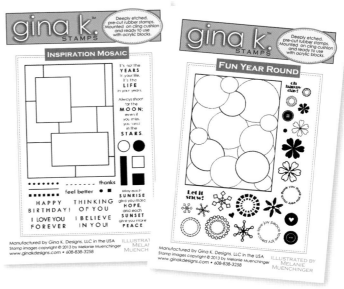

**A Beautiful Life** showcases elegantly arranged tulips surrounding an oval window. This set is perfect for springtime designs, Mother's Day, Easter or any time you need a beautiful card. The oval opening in the frame provides the ideal space for a stamped sentiment or photo. You will love the double border which resembles several layers when stamped. The charming bee and butterfly images can be used to add a touch of nature to your cards or become the perfect stamped embellishment when your card needs just a little something.

**Fun Year Round** is a playful, graphic set with round elements which fit circle punches or dies ranging in size from ½–1¾ inches that can be stamped into a carefully planned frame of layered circles. The open spaces in the frame are ideal for stamping sentiments or framing buttons and other embellishments. You can also use the smaller elements to create patterns with the assistance of a long line in the set that can be stamped to make a grid for easy placement of elements.

**Festive Frame** contains an ornate frame with a spray of pine cones, clusters of pine needles, poinsettias and seven timeless seasonal greetings. This is the perfect set for winter holiday projects. The poinsettias match those found in A Year of Flowers stamp set, giving this set added versatility.

If you love bold stamping techniques and die cutting:

**Branching Out** contains a simple yet elegant frame with leafy branches that work for so many occasions. This set includes three smaller frames—oval, circle and square—which fit more than 50 of the popular Spellbinders™ Nestabilities® die sets and many other brands of dies and punches on the market. While there are no greetings in this set, stamped, sticker or rub-on

sentiments of any kind can be added to these frames. These frames also make terrific tags or focal points when used individually.

**Wild at Heart** is a wonderful bold frame with carved-out flowers and curving stems. The included greetings can be stamped on a separate panel and added directly over the stamped frame.

These precut sets are made from deeply etched red rubber, mounted on cling vinyl and ready to be used with acrylic blocks. Some Gina K. Designs sets are also offered in premium-quality photopolymer, the highest quality clear stamps on the market. Clear photopolymer produces a crisp image like rubber does, but gives you the ability to see through the image, which helps with stamping greetings, frames and other images straight on your cardstock.

Each large frame image measures approximately 4 x 5¼ inches, so you will need a large acrylic block for stamping. A 6 x 6-inch block with gridlines is recommended. This size is easy to hold, and the gridlines help you keep the stamp aligned on your mat. A 4 x 6-inch block will work as well. For the sentiments and smaller images, 2½- and 3½-inch square blocks are appropriate. It is best to use a block that is just slightly larger than your image, as one that is too big can tend to rock and be hard to balance when stamping.

## Electronic Cutting Files

While no cut files are used in this book so that the projects may easily be recreated by anyone, Studio files for the Silhouette cutting machine for all seven of these sets are available for individual purchase in the Gina K. Designs online store. These files cut all the images included in the sets as well as coordinating bonus shapes. For the money, they are an exceptional value and eliminate the need for punches, saving precious time that would be spent cutting out images by hand.

## Additional Materials You Will Also Need

- Black ink pad (or brown if you prefer earthy colors or a vintage look)
- Coloring medium of choice: markers, pencils, watercolors for example
- Smooth, quality cardstock in white or ivory. Ivory usually works best with earthy colors and when a vintage look is desired. White is typically the best choice when working with bright, pastel and jewel tones or if you want a modern, clean design.
- Paper trimmer
- Scoring board or scoring tool for crisp, even folds
- Scissors
- Adhesive and foam dots
- Scratch paper for protecting your work surface and creating masks
- Fun extras: ribbon, buttons, patterned papers, sponges, colored ink pads, glossy cardstock

Patterned papers are so popular in crafting and are available in an endless assortment of styles and colors from a variety of sources. They are used in this book for the popular stamp technique of paper piecing, as well as the less time-consuming faux-paper piecing technique. Custom papers can also be created with small stamp images, which you will learn to do with the coordinating images in these stamp sets. You'll never run out of a favorite "print" this way and can have them in as many colors as you have ink pads!

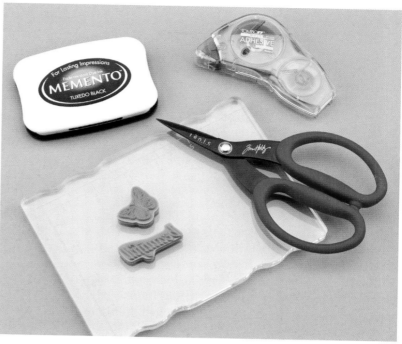

The sample projects that follow use only the seven frame sets, meaning you can re-create more cards exactly with very few sets. As you become more comfortable with the techniques demonstrated, have fun mixing images from the various sets to fill in the frame and expand your design options. These frame stamps are also easily adapted to different looks and types of projects. In addition to cards, consider using these sets on gift bags, jewelry boxes, clock faces, shrink plastic and wrapped candles. Feel free to adapt the stamped frame ideas and techniques covered here to other crafts you love.

Finally, while the completed projects are specific to frame stamp sets from Gina K. Designs, the techniques demonstrated will work with other stamps. The coloring techniques can be used with any line art images and bold techniques with any bold stamps, so you can start applying the techniques right away with other images in your collection. In the end, these frame sets are sure to be some of the most fun and versatile sets in your collection and will produce such amazing results that you will never want—or need—to send out another store-bought card again. *

# Tips, Tricks & Time-Savers

## Creating Card Bases

The frame stamps are designed specifically to be used with A2-size card bases (4¼ x 5½ inches). This is the most common card size used by stampers and paper crafters because one sheet of 8½ x 11-inch cardstock cut in half yields exactly two card bases. These cards require standard postage to mail, have plenty of room to write in and are not too intimidating a space to add designs to for beginner card makers.

### Top-Fold Card Bases

To form a top-fold card base, use a 4¼ x 11-inch piece of cardstock scored at 5½ inches.

### Side-Fold Card Bases

To form a side-fold card base, use a 5½ x 8½-inch piece of cardstock scored at 4¼ inches.

## Prepping the Stamps

For the red rubber stamps, pop out each stamp from the rubber sheet and peel off the paper backing. Clear stamps come on a sheet of clear plastic. Carefully peel each image off the plastic sheet (these will be super sticky the first time but less so after). Next, for both types of stamps, place them on the storage board included with the set. You may want to store this 3-ring punched board in a binder or binder box (available from Gina K. Designs) along with the image sheet for future reference. Some stampers find other storage systems work well for them, but a binder box or container with a lid prevents those tiny images from getting lost. Your stamps are now ready to be used!

Clear stamps can sometimes resist certain inks more than others before the first use due to a slight residue from manufacturing. To get better coverage, you may find it helpful to remove this residue before starting, although it is not always necessary. To do so, simply rub an eraser over the stamp surface and wipe off excess eraser crumbs. Bold images particularly seem to benefit from this type of treatment and produce a more solid image when stamping. You will not need to do this treatment again.

## Adhering Stamps to Blocks & Stamping

Both clear stamps and red rubber stamps mounted on cling foam will cling to a clean acrylic block for stamping, no added adhesive is necessary. Place a large frame stamp onto the 6 x 6-inch block as centered as possible, rather than up against one edge of the block. This will make balancing the block and applying even pressure easier when stamping the image.

Align the top edge of the frame's border along one line of the grid, then after flipping the block over, stamp the frame into a corner of the paper keeping that gridline parallel with the top edge of the cardstock and at a right angle with the side of the paper. Position the stamp anywhere from ⅛ to ½ inch from the cardstock edge to allow for trimming later with either straight or decorative-edge scissors. You'll need to allow more room on the sides to compensate for the different widths of the scissors' cut pattern.

Place the bottom of a sentiment stamp along the middle line on your gridline block. Place images centered over the intersection of the gridlines in the middle. For images that need to touch another stamped image on the paper, such as a flower or leaf coming off a branch, put the bottom edge of the stamp at that intersection. Then center the intersection over where you want the image to touch and stamp.

One of the best advantages to card making with these stamp sets is that four stamped frame images (all from one set or a combination of frames) will fit onto one sheet of cardstock, one in each corner! Simply trim and they are ready to add to four folded card bases, no additional mats are necessary unless you want to add more. This means very little wasted cardstock as well as being able to make four cards in not much more time than it takes to make one. This makes it easy to

have a few extra cards on hand for last-minute needs, without having to get your supplies out again and again to make the same or similar design. A pretty set of handmade cards is also a great gift to give someone!

## Caring for Your Stamps

If you find the stamps are not sticking well to your blocks, simply rinse the stamp and block with water and dry with a rag. A buildup of dirt, dust or lint can create barriers between the two surfaces and hinder the cling. It is a good idea to always keep a damp towel handy to clean stamps between inks and after a stamping session. (A designated rag you can wash is better for the environment than paper towels.) If you don't have time to clean your supplies immediately after use, the good news is they always clean up well later. A heavier buildup of ink may require the use of a stamp-cleaning solution. The many brands offered are inexpensive and intended for stamps so they will not harm the rubber or polymer. With proper care, your stamps will last virtually forever.

## Trimming the Frames

To yield a more professionally finished result, make an effort to keep the width of the border around the stamped frame consistent on all sides. If your design requires more room on one side than another because of the way it will be trimmed or embellished, make the difference in width more noticeable and intentional to prevent it from looking like a mistake. If you find you've trimmed too much off one side, just trim the frame exactly the same on its border edge with a paper cutter or scissors, then layer over colored cardstock mats.

Paper cutters are available in either a sliding or guillotine style. To use, always keep one hand on your paper to hold it in place and the other hand on top of the blade or cutting arm. Holding the mat prevents it from sliding over as the cutter goes through the cardstock, which would result in a less-than-straight cut.

Place stamped paper in the cutter with the frame border parallel to the cutting edge rather than squaring up the cardstock to the bottom edge of the cutter's base. This creates a straight cut even if the frame wasn't perfectly aligned with cardstock edges when stamping. Repeat this process on all sides and the stamped cardstock will have right angles.

Decorative-edge scissors are an inexpensive and easy way to create new and interesting looks! Use the edge of the stamped frame as a guide when cutting to keep the cut pattern even. You can also use a straight-edge ruler and pencil to lightly draw a line to cut along, then erase any visible marks once you've made your cuts. Cut designs such as scallops, postage stamp, zigzag and rickrack are some of the favorite and most versatile to use. Many of the patterns work double duty, creating a different reverse edge when you flip the scissors over.

Dies and cut files for cutting machines are available in so many gorgeous shapes and sizes. Have fun making custom-size frames to suit your specific project, or cut in different shapes if you want something a little different or fancier than a basic rectangle or square.

# Splendid Spotlights
## Your Special Day

Stamp this intricate floral frame tone-on-tone onto colored cardstock for a look that's both subtle and spectacular, or create a gorgeous spotlight design for any season or occasion by coloring and die cutting a portion of the frame to layer over the full image.

**1.** Form a 4¼ x 5½-inch card from aqua cardstock. With card open and laying flat, use light blue ink to stamp frame centered onto card front (Photo 1).

**2.** Clean stamp. Using black ink, stamp frame onto white cardstock. Stamp sentiment onto frame as shown with same color ink (Photo 2).

**3.** Place 2¾ x 3⅞-inch Labels Eight die template over middle of stamped frame; die-cut and emboss (Photo 3).

Photo 1

Photo 2

Photo 3

**tip**

To ensure a crisper stamped image when stamping a frame directly onto a card front, open card and lay flat to allow stamping on a single layer.

## Materials

Gina K. Designs Pure Luxury cardstock: white, ocean mist
Gina K. Designs Arranged with Love stamp set
Imagine Crafts/Tsukineko Memento ink pads: tuxedo black, summer sky
Copic® markers: B12, BG05, G94, R35, R37, Y02, Y15, YG03
Spellbinders™ Labels Eight die templates (#S5-019)
Die-cutting machine
Stamp scrubber
Stamp cleaner
Plaid Enterprises adhesive foam dots

**4.** Color each portion of die-cut image with markers: light green on all leaves; light yellow, lighter red and aqua on flowers (Photo 4).

Photo 5

Photo 4

**5.** Referring to photos, go over areas of the image with darker shades of each color marker (Photo 5).

**6.** Use foam dots to attach colored die cut to card base, lining up image to match. ✳

**tip**

Adding extra layers of color to your images adds richness to your design and makes lighter colors appear to glow.

# Happy Butterflies

Spotlighting is a technique that is used to highlight portions of an image. Here, butterflies stamped over the circles in this frame design provide different sections to color for a whimsical look.

**Materials**
Gina K. Designs Pure Luxury cardstock: white, smoky slate, innocent pink
Gina K. Designs stamp sets: Fun Year Round, A Beautiful Life
Imagine Crafts/Tsukineko Memento ink pads: London fog, angel pink
Copic® marker: R20
Glitter pen
Mark Richards self-adhesive rhinestone
EK Success punches: small corner rounder, 1¼-inch circle, 1⅜-inch circle
Plaid Enterprises adhesive foam dots
Scor-Pal double-sided adhesive

**1.** Form a 5½ x 4¼-inch card from pink cardstock. Punch bottom corners of card using small corner rounder. Cut a 3 x 5½-inch panel from slate gray cardstock; adhere to center of card front.

**2.** Stamp frame in pink onto white cardstock. Cut a ⅛-inch border on all sides. Punch bottom corners with small corner rounder. Stamp butterflies in gray, overlapping circles (Photo 1).

**3.** Using a marker, color in only the portions of the butterfly on one side of the overlapping circles. Trace lines on wings with glitter pen (Photo 2).

Photo 1

Photo 2

**4.** Stamp small and large flowers and bubble burst randomly in pink within other circles on frame to fill in background. Stamp button images in gray as shown. Use pink marker to fill in button centers, circles on burst image and small areas between circles and outer border.

**5.** Stamp round sentiment in gray onto white cardstock and stamp smaller sentiment, also in gray, inside round greeting. Punch a 1¼-inch circle around stamped sentiment piece and a 1⅜-inch circle from pink cardstock. Adhere circles together. Use foam dots to adhere layered circles to frame between butterflies. Attach panel to card front using foam dots.

**6.** Embellish card front as shown with rhinestone. ✳

# Congrats!

Make one part of your image truly special with dramatic coloring. Who can resist a single red rose?

### Materials
Gina K. Designs Pure Luxury cardstock: white, cherry red
Gina K. Designs Arranged with Love stamp set
Imagine Crafts/Tsukineko Memento tuxedo black ink pad
Copic® markers: C3, C5, G99, R30, R59
10 inches May Arts 1¼-inch-wide olive silk ribbon
Plaid Enterprises adhesive foam dots
Scor-Pal ¼-inch-wide double-sided adhesive

**tip**

To achieve the look of a sepia photo, try this design in shades of brown. Using various shades of a color will result in a monochromatic effect.

# Pretty Pencils
## Vintage Birthday

Create the gorgeous look of watercolor with colored pencils and mineral spirits. The blending technique is easy to master, and you'll love the effect of dramatic dark and light tones on your project.

**tip**

Feel free to stop coloring without completing the entire background. The unfinished portions will create the illusion of a faded, but lovely, timeworn piece.

**Materials**

Gina K. Designs Pure Luxury cardstock: ivory, little boy blue, just peachy
Gina K. Designs stamp sets: Arranged with Love, A Beautiful Life
Ink pads: Ranger Distress (antique linen); Imagine Crafts/Tsukineko Memento (summer sky)
Koh-I-Noor Woodless Colored Pencils
Odorless mineral spirits
Blending stumps
17 inches Gina K. Designs ⅜-inch-wide ivory Pure Luxury grosgrain ribbon
Dress It Up buttons: Heirloom collection (#77), pearlescent
Mark Richards clear self-adhesive rhinestones
Spellbinders™ Romantic Rectangles die templates (#S5-090)
Die-cutting machine
Plaid Enterprises: adhesive foam dots, adhesive dots
Scor-Pal ¼-inch-wide double-sided adhesive

**1.** Form a 4¼ x 5½-inch card from peach cardstock; ink edges light brown.

**2.** Using light brown ink, stamp frame onto ivory cardstock. With dark green colored pencil, add color to the areas of the leaves you want to be darkest: inside folds and below where images overlap (Photo 1).

Photo 1

**3.** Dip blending stump into mineral spirits. Begin rubbing wet stump over colored areas, moving in small circles and working toward edges of images to drag color. ***Note:***

*When color stops moving and the stump sounds scratchy on the cardstock, pick up more mineral spirits with the stump* (Photo 2).

Photo 2

**tip**

For a different look, stamp your image using a light-color ink. Light brown is perfect for a vintage project like this one.

**tip**

No thread to match your project? Use tiny slivers of cardstock to thread your buttons for perfect coordination.

Photo 3

Photo 4

**4.** In same manner as before, add color to flowers as desired and blend. Add more color to darker areas if more contrast is needed; blend with mineral spirits and blending stump (Photos 3 & 4).

**5.** Die-cut and emboss a 4 x 5⅛-inch Romantic Rectangle from colored frame.

**6.** Referring to photo and using blue ink, stamp sentiment onto frame.

**7.** Using light brown ink, stamp a butterfly onto ivory cardstock. Color blue and blend in the same manner as before. Cut out and attach to frame using foam dots. Embellish butterfly with rhinestones.

**8.** Adhere frame to a 4 x 5¼-inch piece of blue cardstock. Wrap a 6- inch length of ribbon around top of layered piece; secure ends to back. Adhere to card front.

**9.** Tie a bow from remaining ribbon; trim ends. Cut a thin strip from blue cardstock. Stack two buttons on top of each other; thread cardstock strip through buttonholes; wrap strip around center of bow and adhere to back of bow with adhesive dots. Attach bow to card front as shown in the same manner. ✳

# In the Tulips

Colored pencils and mineral spirits are perfect for creating the soft blended pastels on this baby card. What sweeter way to announce a new baby girl?

Photo Copyright Marian Adrian Photography

To switch to another color on your blending stump, scrape the tip with a sanding block until you've removed all the color from the end.

## Materials

Gina K. Designs Pure Luxury cardstock: ivory, carnival red
Baby photo
Gina K. Designs A Beautiful Life stamp set
Imagine Crafts/Tsukineko Memento tuxedo black ink pad
Koh-I-Noor Woodless Colored Pencils
Black fine-tip marker
Odorless mineral spirits
Blending stump
Mark Richards white self-adhesive pearls
Gina K. Designs pink buttons
7 inches ¾-inch-wide white lace
Spellbinders™ Fancy Tags One die templates (#S4-235)
Die-cutting machine
Craft knife with cutting mat
Plaid Enterprises: adhesive foam dots, adhesive dots
Scor-Pal ¼-inch-wide double-sided adhesive
Computer with printer (optional)

1. Form a 5½ x 4¼-inch card from red cardstock.

2. Stamp frame on ivory cardstock. Cut out frame leaving a ¼-inch border.

3. Using red colored pencil, add color to areas of flowers you want to be darkest. Dip blending stump into odorless mineral spirits and begin blending color, moving stump in small circles.

4. Color leaves and stems green only in areas you want to be darkest. Use opposite end of blending stump to blend in the same manner as before.

5. Using craft knife and cutting mat, cut oval center from frame. Layer and adhere photo and frame together using double-sided adhesive. Wrap lace around bottom edge of layered piece; secure ends to back.

6. Hand-write, or use a computer to generate, baby's name onto ivory cardstock. Die-cut and emboss a ⅞ x 3½-inch Fancy Labels One shape around name. Attach to frame as shown using foam dots, wrapping and securing one end of label to back of frame. Attach frame to card front using foam dots.

7. Embellish card front with pearls and buttons as shown, using adhesive dots as needed. *

**tip**

Consider the shape of the image when coloring. Color in one direction on each section, for example: outward on a leaf in the direction the veins would lead.

# To the Mr. & Mrs.

Coloring with pencils on black or dark cardstock is stunning. With the added contrast of white embossing, the images pop like a painting on black velvet.

**Materials**
Gina K. Designs Pure Luxury cardstock: white, black onyx, blue raspberry
Gina K. Designs Arranged with Love stamp set
Imagine Crafts/Tsukineko ink pads: VersaMark (watermark), Memento (tuxedo black)
Ranger white Superfine embossing powder
Koh-I-Noor Woodless Colored Pencils
Odorless mineral spirits
Blending stumps
13 inches Gina K. Designs Pure Luxury ⅝-inch-wide black stitched ribbon
Spellbinders™ die templates: Labels Twenty (#S5-026), Classic Ovals SM (#S4-112)
Die-cutting machine
Embossing heat tool
Plaid Enterprises adhesive foam dots
Tombow liquid paper adhesive

# Paper Piecing
## Happy Birthday Mosaic

Paper piecing will become a favorite technique due to its simple execution and beautiful results. The mosaic frame allows you to showcase several gorgeous prints perfectly every time with no measuring!

**Materials**

Gina K. Designs Pure Luxury red hot cardstock
Gina K. Designs Pure Luxury Berries and
    Vines Designer patterned paper
Gina K. Designs Inspiration Mosaic stamp set
Imagine Crafts/Tsukineko Memento
    tuxedo black: ink pad, marker
Red button
Red baker's twine
Ribbon: Gina K. Designs 8 inches
    ⅝-inch-wide black stitched; 7 inches
    ⅝-inch-wide black gingham
Scor-Pal ¼-inch-wide double-sided adhesive
Tombow liquid paper adhesive

**1.** Form a 5½ x 4¼-inch card from red cardstock.

**2.** Using black ink, stamp frame onto five complementary pieces of patterned papers.

**3.** Cut out one frame (lightest pattern is preferable), leaving a ⅛-inch border. Stamp greeting onto lower rectangle (Photo 1).

**4.** Carefully cut out one or two blocks from one pattern. Run a black marker along edge of each cut piece anywhere that outline needs a touch-up after trimming (Photo 2). *Note: Do the same with the marker around the large frame to give the mat a finished look.*

**6.** Cut one or two different shapes from remaining patterned paper pieces to fill desired spaces on frame. Ink edges black in the same manner as before. Repeat step 5 with these pieces, leaving a few boxes of large frame open to allow main background print to show (Photo 3).

Photo 1

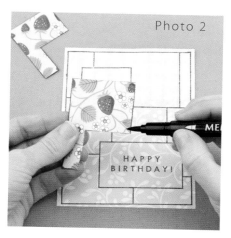

Photo 2

**5.** Position pieces onto main frame before gluing. Choose areas where colors will be opposite from each other to balance layout and keep like patterns from touching.

Photo 3

**7.** When desired look is achieved, add glue to each area on frame, and one at a time, place each cut piece on frame to adhere.

**8.** Wrap one end of gingham ribbon around mosaic frame as shown; secure end to back. Trim remaining end of gingham ribbon and adhere to front of frame as shown. Tie a bow with stitched ribbon; trim ends. Thread baker's twine around bow and through buttonholes; tie knot on front and trim ends. Adhere to mosaic frame as shown. Adhere frame to card front. ✳

**tip**

If your patterned paper has a glossy finish, which sometimes resists ink, try a permanent ink like StazOn when stamping the frame for crisper, darker lines. You can also heat-set the ink to avoid smudging.

# Feel Better Soon

Paper piecing with vibrant cardstock adds rich color and layered dimension to your projects. Flowers trimmed out of the frame make a beautiful get well arrangement.

These frames always look perfect (and perfectly proportioned) in the center of an A2-size card, but offsetting the mat is unexpected and appealing.

## Materials
Gina K. Designs Pure Luxury cardstock: white, carnival blue, jelly bean green, orange
Gina K. Designs Arranged with Love stamp set
Imagine Crafts/Tsukineko Memento tuxedo black ink pad
Copic® marker: Y02
Plaid Enterprises adhesive foam dots
Tombow liquid paper adhesive

**1.** Form a 4¼ x 5½-inch card from orange cardstock.

**2.** Cut a 3⅞ x 5-inch piece from teal cardstock. Stamp frame onto green, orange and white cardstock, reinking each time (Photo 1).

Photo 1

**3.** From green frame, cut away border and all areas of background outside of flowers and leaves. To reach an area surrounded by leaves, cut along leaf line. Center and adhere to teal mat (Photo 2). ***Note:*** *If desired, do not adhere portions of some of the leaves so they can be layered over sentiment panel in step 5.*

Photo 2

**4.** Trim roses from orange stamped frame. Place and adhere over roses on green cut frame, using foam dots as desired to pop-up some roses (Photo 3).

Photo 3

**5.** Using marker, color centers of desired flowers and border of sentiment frame on white stamped frame. Stamp sentiment onto frame as shown (Photo 4).

Photo 4

**6.** Cut out flowers and sentiment frame; adhere to green mat.

**7.** Adhere assembled mat to top corner of card front as shown. ✳

# Let It Snow

Fun patterns like swirls and polka dots are so festive for a snow-themed card, even if they aren't bright white. The repeating dots and stamped snowflakes are enough to evoke the feeling of a good-natured snowball fight!

## Materials

Gina K. Designs Pure Luxury cardstock: white, grass green, carnival red
Gina K. Designs Hello Sunshine patterned paper pack
Gina K. Designs Fun Year Round stamp set
Ink pads: Imagine Crafts/Tsukineko Memento (bamboo leaves); Clearsnap Vivid! (brick)
Mark Richards self-adhesive rhinestones
Green baker's twine
Spellbinders™ Classic Postage Stamp die templates (#E8-005)
Die-cutting machine
Circle punches: 1¼ inch, 1⅜ inch
Plaid Enterprises adhesive foam dots
Tombow liquid paper adhesive

# Faux Paper Piecing
## Beautiful Life Together

Stamp images directly on lighter patterned papers and color for a gorgeous layered look. Color the frame's borders to create the illusion of matted panels without adding bulk to your design.

Wishing
you a
*beautiful*
*life*
together.

## Materials

Gina K. Designs Pure Luxury cardstock: white, carnival blue
Gina K. Designs Sunshiny Day Designer patterned paper pack
Gina K. Designs A Beautiful Life stamp set
Imagine Crafts/Tsukineko Memento tuxedo black ink pad
Copic® markers: B12, BG05, R05, R27, Y38, YG23, YG67
Craft knife with cutting mat
Ranger Stickles iridescent glitter glue
Plaid Enterprises adhesive foam dots
Tombow liquid paper adhesive

**1.** Form a 5½ x 4¼-inch card from blue cardstock.

**2.** Stamp tulip frame onto yellow floral patterned paper. Referring to photo, color image, assuming light source would be coming from above. Trace underneath tulips and leaves with pale aqua marker (Photo 1).

Photo 1

**3.** Color oval rim and rectangle border red. Cut out frame leaving a ⅛-inch border. Color outside edge green (Photo 2).

Photo 2

**4.** Using craft knife and cutting mat, cut out inside oval of frame, cutting around outer edge of tulips (Photo 3).

Photo 3

**5.** Cut a 4⅛ x 5⅜-inch piece from white cardstock. Position frame over white cardstock piece to find proper placement for sentiment. Stamp greeting with black ink inside window (Photo 4).

Wishing
you a
*beautiful
life*
together.

Photo 4

**6.** Stamp one butterfly to the left of the sentiment and one butterfly onto lower left corner of frame. Color butterflies blue. Layer and adhere sentiment panel and frame to card front, making sure to center frame over sentiment panel.

**tip**

Stamp and color image panels as desired before adhering to your project.

**7.** Stamp two more butterflies onto white cardstock and color.

**8.** Cut out butterflies from white cardstock piece, trimming off antennae. Add glitter glue to wings; let dry. Attach butterflies over stamped butterflies on frame using foam dots (Photo 5). ✳

Photo 5

# Season's Greetings

You'll love the homespun look of this cozy Christmas card with its multicolored ginghams. Change the greeting and this design works for fall holidays as well.

## Materials

Gina K. Designs Pure Luxury cardstock: white, honey mustard
Gina K. Designs patterned paper packs: Casual Friday, Petals & Wings
Gina K. Designs Festive Frame stamp set
Ink pads: Imagine Crafts/Tsukineko Memento (rich cocoa); Ranger Distress (antique linen)
Copic® markers: E37, G99, R35
Ranger bisque Liquid Pearls
Brown baker's twine
Tan button
Spellbinders™ Classic Ovals LG die templates (#S4-110)
Die-cutting machine
Sponge dauber
Plaid Enterprises adhesive foam dots
Tombow liquid paper adhesive

1. Form a 5½ x 4¼-inch card from mustard cardstock.

2. Cut a 3⅜ x 4¼-inch piece from pink patterned paper. Adhere to card front as shown.

3. Using dark brown ink, stamp frame onto brown patterned paper. Cut out frame leaving a ⅛-inch border. Color poinsettias red, needles green and pinecones brown. Fill in borders with green marker and outside edge of border with red marker. Adhere frame centered to card base. Dot bisque Liquid Pearls onto centers of flowers. Lay flat to dry.

4. Die-cut and emboss a 3 x 2¼-inch Classic Oval LG from white cardstock; leave die template in place. Sponge light brown ink over edges; remove die template. Using dark brown ink, stamp sentiment centered onto die-cut oval. Attach to card front as shown using foam dots.

5. Cut several 3–4-inch-long skinny strips from patterned papers and red and white cardstock. Referring to photo, hold strips together over front of button. Thread baker's twine through buttonholes from back to front. Tie knot on front, securing paper and cardstock strips in place. Spread strips apart to make a little spray. Trim ends of twine. Adhere button to card as shown. *

# Mother's Day

Many papers today are designed to look just like fabric. Printed canvas, twill, linen or cheesecloth is fabulous to use with stamps and the faux paper-piecing technique.

## Materials
Gina K. Designs Pure Luxury cardstock: carnival red, innocent pink
Gina K. Designs Hello Sunshine patterned paper pack
Gina K. Designs A Beautiful Life stamp set
Imagine Crafts/Tsukineko Memento tuxedo black ink pad
Sakura Stardust Glitter pen
Koh-I-Noor Woodless Colored Pencils
Blending stumps
Odorless mineral spirits
18 inches ⅜-inch-wide red gingham ribbon
Pink pearl stickpin
Making Memories piercing tool
Foam craft mat
Gina K. Designs piercing template
Plaid Enterprises adhesive foam dots
Tombow liquid paper adhesive

Little touches like pierced corners, gingham ribbon and stickpins are reminiscent of sewing and are perfect complements to fabric printed papers.

have a *beautiful Mother's Day!*

I LOVE YOU
FOREVER

# Cool Color Blocks
## Love You Forever

The gradient from several stamped frames is incredibly simple to make but creates vibrant pops of color. Tearing and piecing the sections together is an easy way to add beautiful texture.

**Materials**

Gina K. Designs Pure Luxury cardstock: white, red hot
Gina K. Designs stamp sets: Wild at Heart, Inspiration Mosaic
Imagine Crafts/Tsukineko Memento ink pads: love letter, rose bud, angel pink
Stamp scrubber
Stamp cleaner
Scor-Pal double-sided adhesive

**1.** Form a 4¼ x 5½-inch card from red cardstock.

**2.** Stamp frame three times on white cardstock, once in red, once in hot pink and once in light pink. **Note:** *Clean stamp in between inking.* Cut out each stamped frame leaving a ¼-inch border (Photo 1).

**3.** Adhere light pink frame to card base. Stamp greeting in red on lower right corner.

**4.** Cut off bottom half of red frame. Adhere top part over pink frame lining up top and side edges (Photo 2).

**5.** Tear off top third and bottom third of hot pink frame to reveal a white torn edge on each side. Curl edges up with fingers to create texture. Adhere to middle of frame, lining up stamped images (Photo 3). ✳

Photo 2

Photo 3

Photo 1

# Artful Blocks

The Inspiration Mosaic set contains multiple shapes and a line that allows for creating patterns which are reminiscent of fine art or stained glass. Just add your favorite colors!

## Materials

Gina K. Designs Pure Luxury cardstock:
   white, in the navy, key lime,
   wild lilac, blue raspberry
Sticky notes
Gina K. Designs Inspiration Mosaic stamp set
Clearsnap Vivid inky blue ink pad
Copic® markers: B06, B39, BG01, V17, YG23
Plaid Enterprises adhesive foam dots
Scor-Pal double-sided adhesive

**1.** Form a 5½ x 4¼-inch card from navy blue cardstock.

**2.** Stamp frame onto white cardstock. Cut off bottom frame to make a 4-inch square (Photo 1).

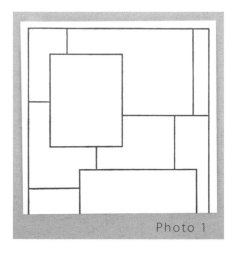

Photo 1

**3.** Mask off boxes with sticky notes and stamp a line perpendicular to masked line (Photo 2).

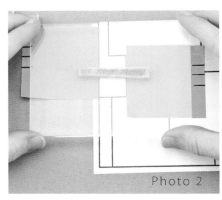

Photo 2

**4.** Repeat, stamping line to create parallel ¼-inch sections, reinking each time (Photo 3). Remove masks.

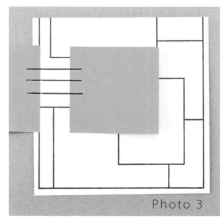

Photo 3

**5.** Move sticky note to mask off additional portions of frame. In the same manner as steps 3 and 4, use stamped lines on masks as guidelines for stamping evenly spaced sections with line stamp (Photo 4).

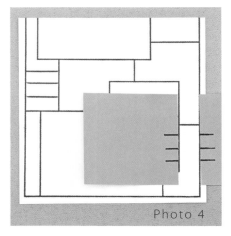

Photo 4

**6.** Mask sides to divide sections outside of border (Photo 5).

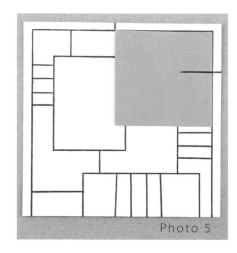

Photo 5

It's not the
**YEARS**
in your life,
it's the
**LIFE**
in your years.

**7.** Stamp open square image across lines in frames to create two divided sections (Photo 6).

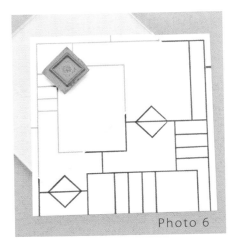

Photo 6

**8.** Color in different portions of grid with markers. Alternate colors so no two same-color sections touch (Photo 7).

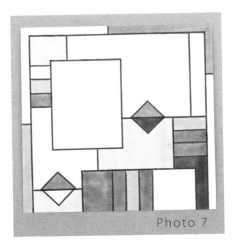

Photo 7

It's not the
**YEARS**
in your life,
it's the
**LIFE**
in your years.

**9.** Cut the following cardstock pieces: 1⅛ x 4-inch purple, 2 x 2½-inch lime, 2⅜ x 1¼-inch turquoise. Adhere to card front as shown (Photo 8).

Photo 8

**10.** Attach colored stamped frame to card front as shown using foam dots.

Stamp the large frame image on several sheets of solid-color cardstock to create unique paper-pieced color-block designs.

**11.** Stamp a frame and sentiment onto white cardstock, stamping sentiment inside rectangle as shown. Cut out sentiment rectangle from frame and attach to card front as shown using foam dots. Stamp one small open square overlapping one of the lines on frame. Color and cut out. Attach to card front as shown using foam dots. ✳

# Hope Is Honey

This card takes inspiration from a popular trend, and the Inspiration Mosaic frame makes color blocking simple with markers or sponging. Use the reverse masking technique to add smaller images to some areas and create a virtual flurry of activity with gorgeous crystal flourishes.

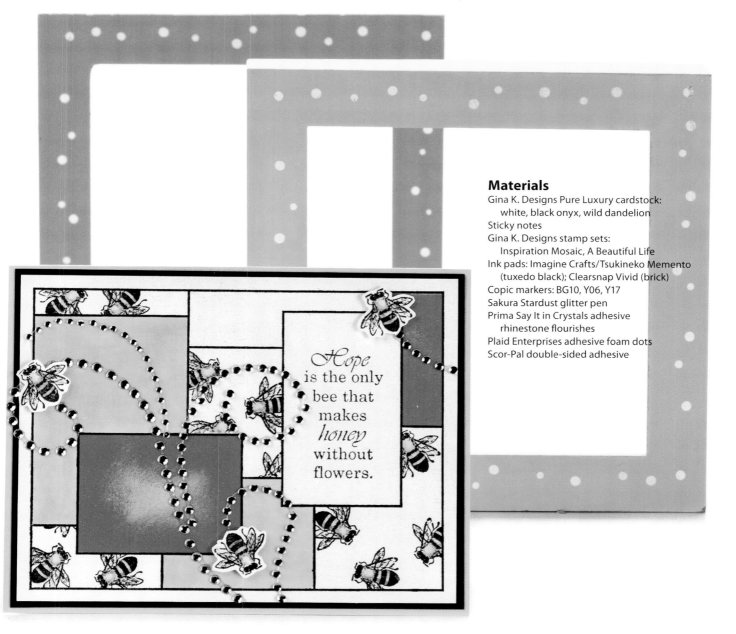

## Materials
Gina K. Designs Pure Luxury cardstock: white, black onyx, wild dandelion
Sticky notes
Gina K. Designs stamp sets: Inspiration Mosaic, A Beautiful Life
Ink pads: Imagine Crafts/Tsukineko Memento (tuxedo black); Clearsnap Vivid (brick)
Copic markers: BG10, Y06, Y17
Sakura Stardust glitter pen
Prima Say It in Crystals adhesive rhinestone flourishes
Plaid Enterprises adhesive foam dots
Scor-Pal double-sided adhesive

# Terrific Two Steps
## Bloom Where You're Planted

Stamp sets with two-step elements allow you to create easy layered designs. Stamping the larger images first and saving the tiniest elements for last will allow you to see where to add a little more color or more stamping for perfect balance.

## Materials

Gina K. Designs Pure Luxury cardstock:
   ivory, dark chocolate, fresh asparagus
Sticky note
Gina K. Designs stamp sets:
   Branching Out, Wild at Heart
Imagine Crafts/Tsukineko Memento ink pads:
   rich cocoa, Morocco, bamboo leaves
Imagine Crafts/Tsukineko Memento
   rich cocoa marker
12 inches ⅜-inch-wide brown/white
   stitched ribbon
Brown baker's twine
Spellbinders™ die templates: Labels Twenty-
   Four (#S4-353), Lacey Squares (#S4-295)
Die-cutting machine
Scor-Bug Embosser
Scor-Buddy
Craft sponge
Plaid Enterprises adhesive foam dots
Tombow liquid paper adhesive

**1.** Form a 4¼ x 5½-inch card from green cardstock. Adhere a 4¼ x 3⅛-inch piece of brown cardstock to card front as shown.

**2.** Stamp frame in brown onto ivory cardstock. Cut out frame leaving a ¼-inch border.

**3.** In the same manner, stamp smaller square frame onto ivory cardstock. Die-cut and emboss a 2½-inch Lacey Square around stamped frame (Photo 1).

Photo 1

**4.** Cover center section of sentiment on stamp with a piece of sticky note. Ink stamp with green ink. Remove sticky note and ink remaining section with brown marker. Huff on sentiment stamp and stamp in center of die-cut square (Photo 2).

Photo 2

**5.** Apply orange ink onto flower stamp; add just a touch of brown to center and bottom with a marker. Stamp flowers at different angles next to branches on both frames, reinking each time (Photo 3).

Photo 3

**6.** Ink berry cluster in green and stamp around leaves on both frames (Photo 4).

Photo 4

**7.** Place large frame on Scor-Buddy with track just outside frame and roll Scor-Bug down edge to create a pierced line. Repeat on all sides (Photo 5).

Photo 5

**8.** Refer to photo and use fine-tip end of marker to connect dots on pierced line border to create a stitched look. Adhere this frame to card front as shown.

**9.** Die-cut a 2⅞-inch Labels Twenty-Four shape from green cardstock; leave die template in place. Ink green and remove die template. Attach to card front as shown using foam dots.

**10.** Wrap ribbon around card front as shown. Wrap a length of baker's twine around ends of ribbon as shown. Tie knot and trim ends of twine and ribbon.

**11.** Adhere sentiment frame to card font as shown using foam dots. ✳

# Thank You Very Much

Fill the circles in this frame with colorful images or your favorite dimensional embellishments! Look around for color inspiration—it's everywhere you look!

## Materials

Gina K. Designs Pure Luxury cardstock: white, wild dandelion, vibrant violet
Gina K. Designs Fun Year Round stamp set
Imagine Crafts/Tsukineko Memento ink pads: tuxedo black, ladybug, dandelion, tangelo, cottage ivy, grape jelly
Imagine Crafts/Tsukineko Memento markers: ladybug, dandelion, tangelo, cottage ivy, grape jelly
Various colored buttons
Red brads
Paper-piercing tool
Plaid Enterprises adhesive foam dots
Tombow liquid paper adhesive

To create a 3-D effect, stamp the image, lift the stamp and shift slightly, then stamp again without reinking. When repeating this technique on a design, always shift the stamp in the same direction so the perspective is consistent.

# Joy

## This quick-to-make card is terrific for everyone on your Christmas list!

### Materials

Gina K. Designs Pure Luxury cardstock: white, ocean mist, red hot, sandy beach
Gina K. Designs stamp sets: Inspiration Mosaic, Festive Frame
Imagine Crafts/Tsukineko ink pads: VersaMark (watermark), Memento (bamboo leaves, ladybug)
Ranger White Opaque pen
Ranger white embossing powder
Red baker's twine
Spellbinders™ Classic Ovals SM die templates (#S4-112)
Die-cutting machine
Embossing heat tool
Plaid Enterprises adhesive foam dots
Tombow liquid paper adhesive

**tip**

Use a white gel pen to add shine to the stamped berries.

Always shoot
for the
**MOON;**
even if
you miss,
you land
in the
**STARS.**

# Serene Scenes
## Shoot for the Moon

Use sponges, ink and scrap paper to create a beautiful, moonlit night scene. The addition of the mosaic frame places the spectacular landscape outside a window.

### Materials
Gina K. Designs Pure Luxury black onyx cardstock
Scrap paper (copy paper)
Gina K. Designs Inspiration Mosaic stamp set
Imagine Crafts/Tsukineko Memento ink pads: tuxedo black, Danube blue, lulu lavender
Ranger White Opaque pen
Spellbinders™ Standard Circles LG die templates (#S4-114)
Die-cutting machine
Sponge daubers
Scor-Pal double-sided adhesive
Repositionable tape

**1.** Form a 4¼ x 5½-inch card from black cardstock.

**2.** Using black ink, stamp mosaic frame onto white cardstock. Cut out frame leaving a ⅜-inch border. In the same manner, stamp sentiment into vertical rectangular area.

**3.** Die-cut a 2⅜-inch Standard Circles LG shape from scrap paper. Place die-cut circle over greeting on frame, masking sentiment.

**4.** Using a clean sponge dauber, sponge lavender ink lightly around die-cut circle (Photo 1).

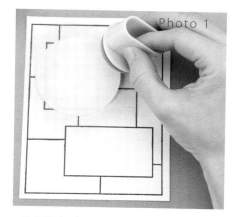
Photo 1

**5.** With die-cut circle still in place and using a clean sponge and blue ink, go over top part of circle around top corners and top half of mat. Remove die-cut circle (Photo 2).

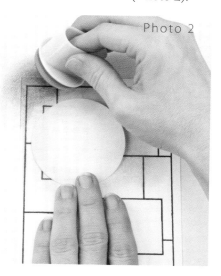
Photo 2

**6.** Place circle about 1½ inches below first circle area you created to make a reflection. Repeat steps 4 and 5 with lavender and blue inks. Remove mask (Photo 3).

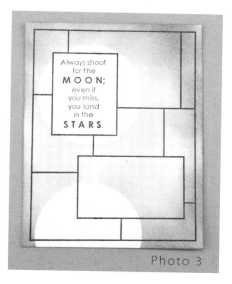

Always shoot
for the
**M O O N;**
even if
you miss,
you land
in the
**S T A R S.**

Photo 3

**7.** Tear off edge from a scrap piece of paper and place below moon; secure in place with repositionable tape. Place straight edge of another sheet of scrap paper just below torn edge to create horizon. Sponge on black ink until you achieve a fairly uniformly dark silhouette (Photo 4).

Photo 4

**8.** Remove top torn mask and shift up just a bit to create a second set of hills. Sponge on more black ink, but not as heavy, to create a more shadowy effect (Photo 5).

Photo 5

**9.** Remove scrap-paper masks. Rotate mat 180 degrees and repeat steps 7 and 8 to create reflected hills. Secure masks in place with repositionable tape and use a lighter touch with ink so reflection is not as dark as first set of hills. ***Note:*** *Place torn mask at same height but flip mask over so reflected hills will mirror the ones directly above; place straight-edge mask along same horizon line.*

**10.** Remove mask.

**11.** Rotate mat so the image is right side up. Using white pen, add dots randomly to sky to create stars. Add a few short, wavy lines randomly on water to create ripples (Photo 6).

Photo 6

**12.** Adhere mat to card base. ✻

When
someone
*you love*
becomes a
*memory,*
the memory
becomes a
*treasure.*

# Treasured Memory

Smaller frames within the Branching Out set create a frame within a frame, appropriate for spotlighting a sentiment. Masking the sentiment and sponging warm colors over the branches suggests a rising or setting sun. The pair of perched birds suggests a quiet, intimate moment.

## Materials

Gina K. Designs Pure Luxury cardstock: white, cranberry tart, black onyx
Scrap paper
Gina K. Designs stamp sets: Branching Out, A Beautiful Life
Imagine Crafts/Tsukineko Memento ink pads: tuxedo black, rhubarb stalk, cantaloupe, tangelo
Sponge daubers
Spellbinders™ Standard Circles SM die templates (#S4-116)
Die-cutting machine
Tombow liquid paper adhesive

**1.** Form a 5½ x 4¼-inch card from black cardstock. Adhere a 5¼ x 3½-inch piece of red cardstock to card front as shown.

**2.** Stamp frame in black on white cardstock; cut out frame leaving a ¼-inch border. Ink circle frame with red ink and stamp image onto scrap paper. Without reinking, stamp image inside frame on white cardstock as shown positioning branches on right side to allow room for greeting on left (Photo 1).

Photo 1

**3.** Sponge yellow ink all over mat, leaving white space (Photo 2).

Photo 2

**4.** Die-cut a 2⅝-inch Standard Circles SM shape from scrap paper, creating a mask. Cover circle frame with mask and sponge orange ink onto frame as shown (Photo 3).

Photo 3

**5.** Leave circle mask in place and sponge red ink onto frame, creating a mottled look and allowing orange and yellow to show through (Photo 4).

Photo 4

**6.** Finish design by adding the two-step elements. Stamp sentiment in black inside circle. Stamp a few black single branches at lower right corner. Stamp flowers in red on vine and on branches inside circle frame, alternating sides of branches and turning flower image as you go. Stamp birds on bottom border to create a perch (Photo 5).

Photo 5

**6.** Adhere frame to card front as shown. ✳

# Sunrise, Sunset

Stamp the Inspiration Mosaic frame over a picture to divide it into smaller canvases and your photo takes on the look of an amazing gallery piece.

Use a permanent ink if stamping directly on a glossy print, or print photos on cardstock if you aren't comfortable stamping on an original.

**Materials**
Gina K. Designs Pure Luxury cardstock: white, smoky slate
Gina K. Designs Inspiration Mosaic stamp set
Imagine Crafts/Tsukineko Memento tuxedo black ink pad
Tombow liquid paper adhesive
Computer with color printer

# Outside the Lines
## Spirit of Christmas

These contrasting Christmas colors fade into one another like a gorgeous watercolor painting. This emboss-resist technique allows you to confidently add color to produce a stylish, yet easy to mass-produce, card—perfect for the holidays!

May the spirit of Christmas bring you *peace*. The gladness of Christmas give you *hope*. The warmth of Christmas grant you *love*.

## Materials

Gina K. Designs Pure Luxury cardstock:
  white, fresh asparagus, cherry red
Gina K. Designs Festive Frame stamp sets
Imagine Crafts/Tsukineko ink pads: VersaMark
  (watermark), Memento (bamboo
  leaves, love letter, rhubarb stalk)
Ranger white embossing powder
Mark Richards white self-adhesive pearls
Spellbinders™ Classic Scalloped Squares
  LG die templates (#S4-127)
Die-cutting machine
EK Success Wave Flourish Punch
Embossing heat tool
Sponge daubers
Paper towels or soft cloth
Plaid Enterprises adhesive foam dots
Tombow liquid paper adhesive

**1.** Form a 4¼ x 5½-inch card from red cardstock.

**2.** Using watermark ink, stamp frame onto white cardstock. Sprinkle with embossing powder, tap off excess and heat-emboss (Photo 1).

Photo 1

**3.** Using red ink, stamp sentiment onto center of frame. Sponge red ink over poinsettias; wipe ink off embossed poinsettias as needed using a paper towel or soft cloth (Photo 2).

Photo 2

**4.** In the same manner as before, sponge olive ink over needles and pinecones (Photo 3).

Photo 3

**5.** Cut out frame leaving a ⅛-inch border.

**6.** Punch flourishes from green cardstock scraps. Adhere punched flourishes to opposite corners of frame with dots of liquid adhesive.

**7.** Die-cut and emboss two 4 x 4-inch Classic Scalloped Squares LG shapes from green cardstock. Line up and adhere die-cut squares to create a scalloped mat (Photo 4).

Photo 4

**8.** Layer and adhere scalloped mat and frame together as shown. Attach to card front using foam dots. Embellish card using self-adhesive pearls. ✳

# Just for Being You

Sponging soft pastel color over a white embossed image produces a dreamy quality, like looking at flowers through frosted glass. Use darker colors for a bolder look.

## Materials
Gina K. Designs Pure Luxury cardstock:
  white, lovely lavender
Gina K. Designs Arranged with Love stamp set
Imagine Crafts/Tsukineko ink pads:
  VersaMark (watermark), Memento
  (pear tart, lulu lavender, grape jelly)
Ranger white embossing powder
Mark Richards 3mm white self-adhesive pearls

6½ inches Gina K. Designs Pure Luxury
  ribbons: ⅝-inch-wide white organza,
  ¼-inch-wide green grosgrain
Spellbinders™ Labels Twenty die
  templates (#S5-026)
Die-cutting machine
Embossing heat tool
Sponge dauber
Paper towels or soft cloth
Plaid Enterprises adhesive foam dots
Scor-Pal double-sided adhesive

**1.** Form a 5½ x 4¼-inch card from lavender cardstock.

**2.** Using watermark ink, stamp frame onto white cardstock. Sprinkle with embossing powder, tap off excess and heat-emboss.

**3.** Referring to photo and using a sponge dauber, apply green ink over leaves on frame, rubbing gently in circles while inking. Wipe ink off embossed poinsettias as needed using paper towel or soft cloth. Repeat until desired look is achieved.

**4.** In the same manner and using a new sponge dauber, ink flowers lavender.

**5.** Cut out frame, leaving a ¼-inch border.

**6.** Die-cut and emboss a 3¼ x 2¼-inch Labels Twenty shape from lavender cardstock; leave die template in place. Ink die cut lavender; remove die template. In the same manner, die-cut and emboss a 2⅛ x 1½-inch label from white cardstock; in the same manner as before, ink die cut lavender. Using lavender ink, stamp sentiment onto white cardstock label.

**7.** Attach lavender label to middle of frame with adhesive dots.

**8.** Attach a length of double-sided adhesive to back of grosgrain ribbon. Remove backing from adhesive and adhere grosgrain ribbon to center of organza ribbon. Wrap layered ribbon around frame, securing ends to back.

**9.** Referring to photo, attach sentiment label to frame using foam dots. Adhere frame to card front.

**10.** Embellish card with self-adhesive pearls as shown. ✳

# Sweet Boy

The Fun Year Round frame makes adding photos to your project a snap! Use a large photo as the focal point, or create a collage using several photos placed in the circles around the frame.

## Materials
Gina K. Designs Pure Luxury cardstock: white, ocean mist, turquoise sea, little boy blue
Gina K. Designs Fun Year Round stamp set
Imagine Crafts/Tsukineko ink pads: Memento (new sprout, summer sky), VersaMark (watermark), StazOn (azure)
Copic® marker: B02
Gray baker's twine
Gina K. Designs buttons: white, aqua, green
Sponge daubers
Plaid Enterprises: adhesive foam dots, adhesive dots
Tombow liquid paper adhesive
Computer with printer

**tip**

Print photos in black and white on regular cardstock, then use a marker or colored pencil to lightly tint select areas. Here, a marker was used to add color to the eyes to bring out those baby blue peepers.

# Direct to Paper
## Thinking of You

Pair up the Inspiration Mosaic stamp set with the faux woodgrain technique to create the look of rich wooden tiles. It's the perfect combo for masculine card designs!

## Materials

Gina K. Designs Pure Luxury
    cardstock: kraft, black onyx
Gina K. Designs stamp sets:
    Inspiration Mosaic, Branching Out
Ink pads: Imagine Crafts/Tsukineko
    Memento (tuxedo black); Ranger
    Distress (vintage photo)
Spellbinders™ Classic Squares LG
    die templates (#S4-126)
Die-cutting machine
Sponge dauber
Plaid Enterprises adhesive foam dots
Tombow liquid paper adhesive

**1.** Form a 5½ x 4¼-inch card from kraft cardstock.

**2.** Using black ink, stamp frame onto two pieces of kraft cardstock, reinking between stamping.

**3.** With long edge of frame horizontal on work surface, drag brown ink pad across stamped frame to create streaks (Photo 1).

Photo 1

Save the cut pieces from
this design to create a
second, unique project.

**4.** With short edge of second frame horizontal on work surface, drag brown ink pad across stamped frame to create streaks (Photo 2).

Photo 2

**5.** Cut out first frame leaving a ⅛-inch border. Adhere to black cardstock; trim a small border.

**6.** Cut out two rectangle panels from remaining stamped frame. **Note:** *If desired, retain rest of frame to use on Beautiful Day card on page 51* (Photo 3).

Photo 3

**7.** Adhere both rectangles from step 6 to black cardstock; trim small borders.

**8.** Referring to photo and using foam dots, attach rectangles to frame from step 5 (Photo 4).

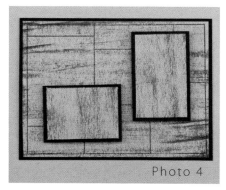

Photo 4

**9.** Using black ink, stamp square frame with branches onto kraft cardstock. Die-cut and emboss a 2½-inch Classic Squares LG shape around stamped image. Leave die template in place; ink corners of die cut brown as shown; remove die template (Photo 5).

Photo 5

**10.** Using black ink, stamp sentiment onto die-cut square. Adhere to black cardstock; trim a small border. Attach to frame as shown using foam dots.

**11.** Using black ink, stamp a small square onto lower right corner of frame. Adhere frame to card front. ✳

# Celebrate the Season

Create the look of whitewashed wood using white or ivory ink and neutral-color paper with natural fibers. Swipe white ink on your paper first, and then repeat with a tan ink to create color variety and intensify the woodgrain illusion.

## Materials

Gina K. Designs Pure Luxury cardstock: dust sage, sandy beach, ivory
Gina K. Designs Festive Frame stamp set
Ink pads: Clearsnap ColorBox pigment (cream white); Imagine Crafts/Tsukineko Memento (pistachio); Ranger Distress (antique linen)
Mark Richards white self-adhesive pearls
EK Success Fancy Photo Corner punch
Spellbinders™ die templates: Classic Ovals SM (#S4-112), Floral Ovals (#S4-356)
Die-cutting machine
Plaid Enterprises adhesive foam dots
Tombow liquid paper adhesive

**1.** Form a 4¼ x 5½-inch card from green cardstock. Adhere a 4 x 5¼-inch piece of white cardstock to card front as shown.

**2.** Cut a 4½ x 6-inch piece from cream cardstock. Drag cream white ink pad across cardstock piece several times. In the same manner, drag light brown ink pad across cardstock piece.

When creating the woodgrain effect, work from light to dark to prevent dirtying your light color ink pad with a darker ink not yet absorbed into the paper.

**3.** Using green ink, stamp frame onto inked cardstock panel.

**4.** Cut out frame, leaving a ⅛-inch border.

**5.** Die-cut and emboss a 2 x 2⅝-inch Classic Ovals SM shape from center oval of frame. Using green ink, stamp sentiment onto cardstock oval to create sentiment panel.

**6.** Die-cut and emboss a 2⅝ x 3⅜-inch Fancy Ovals shape from green cardstock.

**7.** Referring to photo, adhere frame to card front. Using foam dots, layer and attach fancy die-cut oval and sentiment oval to card front.

**8.** Using light brown ink, stamp frame onto ivory cardstock. Cut out upper right and lower left poinsettias from frame. Attach to card front as shown using foam dots.

**9.** Punch a decorative corner from ivory cardstock. Attach to lower

Trimming images from the corners of the stamped frame are perfect embellishments to dress up the opposite open corners.

right corner of card front using foam dots. Embellish card with pearls as desired. ✳

# Beautiful Day

Reassemble the cut pieces from your first faux woodgrain project to create a completely different design with an artsy, clean style. The addition of vibrant tulips is like stepping out into a spring day!

## Materials

Gina K. Designs Pure Luxury cardstock: black onyx, kraft, white, lemon drop, key lime
Gina K. Designs stamp sets: Inspiration Mosaic, A Beautiful Life
Ink pads: Ranger Distress (vintage photo); Imagine Crafts/Tsukineko Memento (tuxedo black, new sprout)
Copic® markers: BV13, RV25, RV55, V17, Y08, Y11, YG03, YG67
Spellbinders™ Classic Rectangles SM die templates (#S4-130)
Die-cutting machine
Plaid Enterprises adhesive foam dots
Tombow liquid paper adhesive

To create this card, use frame retained from Thinking of You card on page 48.

**tip**

Repeat shapes throughout your project with both stamped images and embellishments to create a harmonious design. Here the buttons, silver nailheads on the butterflies and stamped circles on the frame and border all work together.

hello
*beautiful*

# Direct to Stamp
## Hello Beautiful

Bold, shaped stamps are perfect for the kissing technique, as well as for making patterns and borders. Here, a circle stamp used to create a border adds a graphic element, while the butterflies add an airy sweetness to the elegant floral frame.

### Materials
Gina K. Designs Pure Luxury cardstock: white, lovely lavender, wild lilac
Gina K. Designs stamp sets: Wild at Heart, A Beautiful Life, Inspiration Mosaic
Imagine Crafts/Tsukineko Memento ink pads: lulu lavender, sweet plum, grape jelly
Mark Richards silver self-adhesive nailheads
White buttons
Plaid Enterprises: adhesive foam dots, adhesive dots

*Project note: Reink stamps between stamping the same image multiple times.*

**1.** Form a 5½ x 4¼-inch card from lovely lavender cardstock. Using lavender ink, stamp frame centered onto card front.

**2.** Using sweet plum ink, stamp a row of circles onto card front as shown. ***Note:*** *If desired, use a ruler and pencil to lightly draw a straight line to use as a guide before stamping circles* (Photo 1).

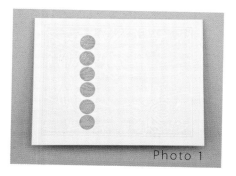

Photo 1

**3.** Ink up frame stamp using lulu lavender ink. Using sweet plum ink, randomly stamp circles directly onto inked frame stamp. Using grape jelly ink, randomly stamp butterflies onto inked frame stamp, turning stamp at a different angle for each butterfly. ***Note:*** *Leave a space to stamp sentiment onto panel* (Photo 2).

Photo 2

**4.** Huff on stamp to remoisten ink and stamp onto white cardstock (Photo 3).

Photo 3

**5.** Referring to photo, trim frame panel down to a 3⅝ x 3⅞-inch piece. Using grape jelly ink, stamp sentiment onto panel. Adhere to card front as shown.

**6.** Using grape jelly ink, stamp two butterflies onto purple cardstock; cut out. Adhere nailheads to butterflies' bodies as shown. Bend wings of butterflies up and attach to card front as shown using foam dots.

**7.** Attach buttons to card front using adhesive dots. ✳

**tip**

Always ink the stamp with lightest colors first and finish with the darkest, so as not to muddy or stain your lighter ink pads. Keep in mind that color-block designs created directly on stamps will be reversed when applied to paper.

# Color Gradient

Swipe various ink pads across the bold stamp and watch as flowers magically emerge when stamped on paper!

## Materials
Gina K. Designs Pure Luxury cardstock: glossy white, sweet mango
Gina K. Designs stamp sets: Wild at Heart, Inspiration Mosaic
Imagine Crafts/Tsukineko Memento ink pads: rich cocoa, lady bug, tangelo
Scor-Pal double-sided adhesive

**1.** Form a 4¼ x 5½-inch card from orange cardstock.

**2.** Cut a 4 x 5¼-inch panel from glossy cardstock.

**3.** Referring to photo and with long edge of stamp horizontal on work surface, drag orange ink pad vertically down what will be bottom section of stamped image, starting just below and ending just above border of stamp. Use a soft cloth or paper towel to wipe ink off border of stamp as needed.

**4.** In the same manner, ink middle of stamp using red ink, overlapping orange area slightly.

**5.** Repeat process using brown ink pad and inking top section of stamp.

**6.** Huff on stamp to moisten and reactivate ink and press stamp onto glossy cardstock panel. Press all over to get good coverage and transfer all the inked detail; carefully remove stamp.

**7.** Using brown ink, stamp sentiment onto panel as shown. Adhere panel to card front. ✳

# Wildflowers

Sanding and tearing the edges of cardstock creates casual textures that are a lovely contrast to the more formal pearls and silk bow.

**Materials**
Gina K. Designs Pure Luxury cardstock:
   glossy white, sandy beach, kraft, dusty sage
Gina K. Designs stamp sets: Wild at Heart, Branching Out
Ranger Distress ink pads: antique linen, vintage photo
Mark Richards white self-adhesive pearls
19 inches May Arts 1¼-inch-wide light brown silk ribbon
Spellbinders™ Grommet Tags die templates (#S4-322)
Die-cutting machine
Sanding block
Plaid Enterprises adhesive foam dots
Scor-Pal double-sided adhesive

**tip**

To ensure you have good coverage of the entire frame, tilt stamp toward the light which will quickly reveal any areas that are still dry and need ink.

May all your weeds be *wildflowers*

# Magic With Markers
## Beautiful Friend

Graceful blades of grass magically appear when you draw on this bold frame stamp with markers! You will love adding your own personal touch to the image with this fun technique and creating one-of-a-kind designs every time.

### Materials
Gina K. Designs Pure Luxury cardstock: white, jelly bean green
Gina K. Designs Wild at Heart stamp set
Imagine Crafts/Tsukineko Memento ink pads: tuxedo black, pear tart
Markers: Imagine Crafts/Tsukineko Memento (bamboo leaves, cottage ivy); Copic® (R20, R37)
Ranger Stickles crystal glitter glue
Plaid Enterprises adhesive foam dots
Tombow liquid paper adhesive

**1.** Form a 4¼ x 5½-inch card from green cardstock.
**2.** Ink up frame using light green ink (Photo 1).

Photo 1

**3.** Using brush tip of bamboo leaves marker and beginning at bottom edge of inked frame below flowers and stems, pull marker up in long, flicking strokes to create blades of grass. Vary height and angle of each stroke for variety to mimic randomness of growing grass. Repeat with cottage ivy marker to add depth (Photo 2).

Photo 2

**4.** Using edge of cottage ivy marker, carefully ink edge of frame stamp (Photo 3).

Photo 3

**5.** Huff on stamp to moisten ink and stamp onto white cardstock. Cut out frame leaving a ⅛-inch border (Photo 4).

Photo 4

**6.** Apply dots of glitter glue onto flower centers and over tiny white dots on frame; let dry and adhere to card front (Photo 5).

**7.** Using black ink, stamp sentiment onto white cardstock. Referring to photo, cut a rectangle around sentiment and V-notch one short edge. Attach to card front using foam dots.

Photo 5

**8.** Using black ink, stamp two butterflies onto white cardstock. Color with light pink marker; layer darker pink near centers, flicking marker outwards. Add glitter glue to wings; let dry. Cut out butterflies, bend wings and adhere to card front as shown using foam dots. ✳

# Etched Marble

Use markers to draw patterns on a bold stamp that resemble the veins or variations in marble or granite. This technique is terrific for masculine cards!

Conserve papers and ribbon where layers in a design overlap by eliminating the portion that would be covered by a mat or tag. The short embossed border used for this card was cut and placed on the card front to make it appear as though it runs all the way across.

## Materials

Gina K. Designs Pure Luxury cardstock: white, smoky slate, little boy blue
Gina K. Designs stamp sets: Wild at Heart, Inspiration Mosaic
Imagine Crafts/Tsukineko Memento London fog ink pad
Imagine Crafts/Tsukineko Memento markers: tuxedo black, Paris dusk
Spellbinders™ Classic Rectangles SM die templates (#S4-130)
Provo Craft Cuttlebug Herringbone embossing folder (#37-1915)
Die-cutting machine
Plaid Enterprises adhesive foam dots
Tombow liquid paper adhesive

**1.** Form a 4¼ x 5½-inch card from gray cardstock.

**2.** Ink up frame stamp using gray ink pad.

**3.** Using blue marker, fast strokes and light pressure, draw crisscrossing, random curving lines onto inked frame stamp. Tap quickly in random spots with brush tip. **Note:** *Drawing lines too carefully and precisely will not look natural.*

**4.** Repeat step 3 with brush tip end of black marker. Using edge of black marker, carefully ink edge of frame stamp.

**5.** Huff on stamp to moisten ink and stamp onto white cardstock. Cut out frame leaving a small border; adhere to card front.

**6.** Cut a 1 x 5½-inch strip from blue cardstock. Emboss with embossing folder. Adhere to card front as shown.

**7.** Stamp sentiment and dotted border onto white cardstock. Die-cut and emboss a 2⅛ x 1⅝-inch Classic Rectangles SM shape around sentiment. Cut a 1⅝ x 2-inch piece from gray cardstock. Layer and adhere sentiment die cut and gray rectangle together as shown. Attach to card front using foam dots. ✳

# Wait on the Lord

Trace the flowers and stems on this stamp with markers to make them pop and embellish your project with individual cut-out blossoms to complete the design.

## Materials

Gina K. Designs Pure Luxury cardstock: pure white, blue raspberry, sweet corn, fresh asparagus
Gina K. Designs Wild at Heart stamp set
Imagine Crafts/Tsukineko Memento ink pads: Bahama blue, summer sky, bamboo leaves, tangelo
Imagine Crafts/Tsukineko Memento markers: Bahama blue, summer sky, bamboo leaves, tangelo
Spellbinders™ die templates: Floral Flourishes (#S4-327), Splendid Circles (#S4-354)
Die-cutting machine
Fiskars Stamp Paper Edgers scissors (#12-92117897)
Sponge daubers
Plaid Enterprises adhesive foam dots
Tombow liquid paper adhesive

# Easy Elements
## Oh Happy Day!

Small elemental stamps provide endless opportunities for creating your own patterns. Enjoy selecting just the right colors and images for your project to build completely unique background papers for any occasion.

***Project note:*** *Reink stamps between stamping multiple images.*

**1.** Form a 4¼ x 5½-inch card from light blue cardstock. Using corner rounder, round lower right corner.

**2.** Cut a 3½ x 5¼-inch piece from navy blue cardstock. Using dark blue ink, stamp multiple buttons along left edge of navy blue panel. Attach to card front using foam dots.

**3.** Cut a 3¼ x 5⅛-inch panel from white cardstock. With long edge horizontal, place panel centered on ruled craft mat positioning panel so a line from craft mat is ½ inch from left edge of white panel (Photo 1).

**4.** Attach long line stamp onto gridline acrylic block. Beginning at center of white cardstock piece and using lines on craft mat as a guide and light blue ink, stamp

vertical lines onto piece, 1 inch apart (Photo 2).

**5.** Rotate cardstock panel so short edge is horizontal on craft mat. In the same manner, using lines of craft mat as a guide and starting at center of piece, stamp lines vertically onto piece 1 inch apart, creating a grid pattern (Photo 3).

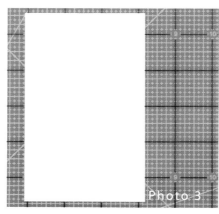

**6.** Using light blue ink, stamp large flowers on every other intersection of lines (Photo 4).

**7.** Using dark blue ink, stamp smaller flowers on top of larger flowers (Photo 5).

## Materials

Gina K. Designs Pure Luxury cardstock: white, little boy blue, in the navy, cherry red

Gina K. Designs Fun Year Round stamp set

Imagine Crafts/Tsukineko Memento ink pads: summer sky, nautical blue, rhubarb stalk

Punches: Uchida (Clever-Lever Super Jumbo Flower); EK Success (small corner rounder); 1¼-inch circle, 1⅜-inch circle

Gina K. Designs Pure Luxury buttons: blue, gray

Whisker Graphics air mail baker's twine

Gina K. Designs acrylic block with gridlines

Scor-Pal Scor-Mat

Plaid Enterprises adhesive foam dots

Tombow liquid paper adhesive

**8.** Stamp large circle bursts in between each flower as shown with red ink. Stamp buttons onto centers of red bursts with dark blue ink (Photo 6).

**9.** Round lower right corner of stamped panel. Attach to card front with foam dots.

**10.** Using red ink, stamp circle burst onto red cardstock. Using navy dark blue ink, stamp sentiment

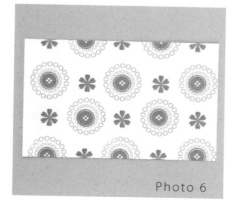

Photo 6

centered onto circle burst on red cardstock. Punch a 1¼-inch circle around stamped image. Punch a 1⅜-inch circle from white cardstock and a flower from navy blue cardstock. Layer and adhere punched pieces together as shown. Attach to card front using foam dots.

**11.** Thread baker's twine through buttons. Tie knots or bows on fronts of buttons; trim ends. Adhere buttons to card front as shown. ✻

# Sending Prayers

Often simple is best. Stamp a basic shape, enhance it with a decorative motif and embellish with pearls to add a touch of class. Change the color scheme and sentiment and you have a beautiful wedding card.

## Materials

Gina K. Designs Pure Luxury cardstock: ivory, honey mustard
Gina K. Designs stamp sets: Branching Out, Arranged with Love
Imagine Crafts/Tsukineko Memento ink pads: pistachio, peanut brittle, rich cocoa
Mark Richards white self-adhesive pearls
Spellbinders™ Classic Squares SM die templates (#S4-128)
Provo Craft Cuttlebug Grace's Frame embossing folder (#20-00217)
Die-cutting machine
1⅜-inch square punch
Stamp scrubber
Stamp cleaning solution
Gina K. Designs acrylic block with gridlines
Scor-Pal Scor-Mat
Plaid Enterprises adhesive foam dots
Tombow liquid paper adhesive

**1.** Form a 5½ x 4¼-inch card from honey mustard cardstock.
**2.** Cut a 4 x 5¼-inch piece from ivory cardstock. Place panel onto craft mat centered between ruled lines. Using green ink, stamp frame onto panel as shown using grid lines as a guide (Photo 1).

Photo 1

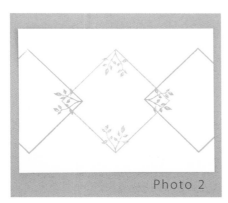

Photo 2

creating a small diamond shape in between frames. Repeat, stamping on opposite side of original stamped frame (Photo 2).

**4.** Center ivory panel inside embossing folder and run through die-cutting machine.

**5.** Using brown ink, stamp sentiment onto ivory cardstock. Die-cut and emboss a 1¼-inch Classic Squares SM shape around sentiment. Punch a 1⅜-inch square from honey mustard cardstock. Layer and adhere squares together; attach to card front as shown using foam dots.

**3.** Clean stamp. Using honey mustard ink, stamp another frame onto panel as shown, overlapping stamped frame from step 2 and

**tip**

Embossed textures look gorgeous over the stamped frame mats. Be sure to do all stamping before embossing, as the embossed areas will not pick up parts of an inked image properly.

**6.** Embellish card with pearls as shown. ✳

# Beautiful Birthday

### Sometimes the smallest details make the biggest impact. Gluing seed beads over stamped berries and butterflies adds a precious quality to this understated design.

**Materials**
Gina K. Designs Pure Luxury
   sweet corn cardstock
Gina K. Designs stamp sets:
   Branching Out, A Beautiful Life
Imagine Crafts/Tsukineko ink pads:
   VersaMark (watermark), Memento
   (rich cocoa, angel pink)
Copic® markers: BG10, BG34,
   E93, R32, YG11, YG23
Sakura Stardust glitter pen
Ranger clear embossing powder
Gina K. Designs Pure Luxury button
Pink seed beads
Brown baker's twine
Embossing heat tool
Plaid Enterprises: adhesive foam
   dots, adhesive dots
Tombow liquid paper adhesive

# Buyer's Guide

**Clearsnap Inc.**
(800) 448-4862
www.clearsnap.com

**Copic®/Imagination International Inc.**
(541) 684-0013
www.copicmarker.com

**Dress It Up**
www.jessejamesbeads.com

**Gina K. Designs**
(608) 838-3258
www.ginakdesigns.com

**EK Success**
www.eksuccessbrands.com

**Imagine Crafts/Tsukineko**
(425) 883-7733
www.imaginecrafts.com

**Koh-I-Noor**
www.kohinoorusa.com

**Making Memories**
(800) 286-5263
www.makingmemories.com

**Mark Richards Enterprises Inc.**
(888) 901-0091
www.markrichardsusa.com

**May Arts Ribbon**
(203) 637-8366
www.mayarts.com

**Plaid Enterprises Inc.**
(800) 842-4197
www.plaidonline.com

**Prima Marketing Inc.**
(909) 627-5532
www.primamarketinginc.com

**Provo Craft**
(800) 937-7686
www.provocraft.com

**Ranger Industries Inc.**
(732) 389-3535
www.rangerink.com

**Sakura of America**
www.sakuraofamerica.com

**Scor-Pal Products**
(877) 629-9908
www.scor-pal.com

**Spellbinders™ Paper Arts**
(888) 547-0400
www.spellbinderspaperarts.com

**Tombow USA**
www.tombowusa.com

**Uchida of America Corp.**
(800) 541-5877
www.uchida.com

**Whisker Graphics**
www.whiskergraphics.com

*The Buyer's Guide listings are provided as a service to our readers and should not be considered an endorsement from this publication.*

---

## Fabulous Stamped Frames

**EDITOR** Tanya Fox

**CREATIVE DIRECTOR** Brad Snow

**PUBLISHING SERVICES DIRECTOR** Brenda Gallmeyer

**MANAGING EDITOR** Brooke Smith

**GRAPHIC DESIGNER** Nick Pierce

**COPY SUPERVISOR** Corene Painter

**SENIOR COPY EDITOR** Emily Carter

**COPY EDITOR** Rebecca Detwiler

**TECHNICAL EDITOR** Corene Painter

**PHOTOGRAPHY SUPERVISOR** Tammy Christian

**PHOTO STYLISTS** Tammy Liechty, Tammy Steiner

**PHOTOGRAPHY** Matthew Owen

**PRODUCTION ARTIST SUPERVISOR** Erin Brandt

**SENIOR PRODUCTION ARTIST** Nicole Gage

**PRODUCTION ASSISTANTS** Marj Morgan, Judy Neuenschwander

ISBN: 978-1-59635-579-8

1 2 3 4 5 6 7 8 9